Chasing Destiny: A Four Week Devotional
Copyright © 2021 Neysa Lewis

All rights reserved. No part of this book may be reproduced in any form or by any electronic or mechanical means, including information storage and retrieval systems, without permission in writing from the publisher, except by reviewers, who may quote brief passages in a review.

Unless otherwise stated, Scripture is taken from King James Version of The Holy Bible.

Also used: The Holy Bible, New International Version (NIV), copyright © 1973, 1978, 1984 by International Bible Society.

ISBN: 978-1-7377587-0-9

www.ladynlewis.com

For speaking engagements or bulk orders, please email
info@ladynlewis.com
Facebook: Lady-Neysa Lewis
Instagram: @ladynlewis
Twitter: @ladynlewis

Cover Design by Danielle Alysse Martin
Self-published via The CAMDA Company
Instagram: @thecamdacompany

I would like to dedicate this to YOU!

Yes, to you, because you have made the decision to seek after, run after, and obtain the destiny that was meant for you. You have made the decision that, at all costs, you are ready to chase your determined end.

Therefore, stand up and make your way to the starting line… on your mark, get set, GO!

Contents...

Week One	25
Week Two	41
Week Three	57
Week Four	71

FOREWORD

Ericka Deshaun, Pastor
Author of A Single Confession

I walked into the Pastor's and First Lady's conference in Cleveland, Ohio with blue hair, fresh kicks, and a fragile heart, which was locked up under maximum security. I had masterfully camouflaged my fear of rejection with eloquent, bold speech, well-crafted words, a bright smile, and southern charisma. Although I seemed to be very outgoing, I was really a low-key introvert. I had experienced a great deal of people hurt and was surviving traumatic experiences that were on a hush. I'm a living testimony you can be the walking wounded while appearing to live well. I had come prepared for any level of rejection. I braced myself with walls that I was convinced were fortified, that is until Lady Neysa Lewis, the author of this amazing devotion, came up to me and after a long pause she said, "I just love you". I felt the sincerity of her words and somehow, I knew she understood exactly where I was. Years later, I've come to know it is true; she has walked and survived her own levels of trauma. Sometimes on our road to destiny, it is bumpy, and it requires an intentional systematic approach to soul care.

Chasing Destiny is an inspiring yet challenging book that calls you to action, to do the necessary work to find your destiny. This devotional is packed with weekly goals which get broken down into daily questions, so you don't feel alone in this journey. It reminds you of who you are because sometimes, while doing the work to become whole, the enemy whispers how we are unworthy, which can discourage you. However, Chasing Destiny is literally about going even when you don't want to.

In a unique way, Lady Neysa has grasped that we often need a step-by-step guide on how to identify our calling and walk in it with confidence. She has found that giving yourself daily tasks, along with motivational reminders of who you are, makes a difference. She has found a way to make this growing process feel attainable. This devotional was strategically written with all of God's people in mind, no matter where you are on your journey.

I want to emphasize a couple of places in this devotional. In Week One: I am Called, we are talking about Sarah. She got the call, which was the promise. However, when it wasn't on her timeline, she manipulated this situation to make an heir, which was never the call. Then Lady Neysa gives us what the call is and how to know you are being called. Listen, if this was out when I was beginning my destiny walk, it would've helped me narrow my aim much more because Lady Neysa was so thorough. Towards the end of week one, we get interactive. She gives you daily questions to prepare for the race.

This devotion is packed with knowledge, nevertheless throughout the book, Lady Neysa continuously calls you to pray. Throughout this devotional every week, there is a prayer. In Preparation for the Race, you ponder and pray on questions. I wanted to point this out because Lady Neysa sees the importance of prayer and always wants to bring us back to a place of intimacy with God. Because there is no way to chase your destiny without the author of life guiding, leading, and directing your path.

It is with great delight I endorse Chasing Destiny as a challenging yet motivational devotional to be fervent about your calling. I look forward to more coming from Lady Neysa Lewis to strengthen God's body.

ACKNOWLEDGEMENTS

I want to first give thanks to God for allowing this devotional to come to fruition. I want to thank my husband for standing beside me and allowing me to heal and work through my anxiety and fear. I am grateful and I love you, Sir! To my children, Brandun, Jaylaan, Ajianna, Amron and Ayden. You make me want to be a better mother and I am proud you call me Mom and I love you guys!

I am so blessed and humbled to have a wonderful church family who supports me. Bread of Life Ministry I love you dearly. Women of Victory, my jewels, I thank you for allowing me to speak into your lives, for allowing me to assist in and mold you into your purpose. Chase Destiny, ladies!!

I also want to thank my spiritual parents, Dr. R. A. and Dr. Victory Vernon for your continuous guidance, teachings and, most importantly, the love you have shown. The Shepherd's Connection for the genuine sisterhood bond that's available and I thank those of you that help support this work through slight pushing and encouragement. I love you more!!

INTRODUCTION

We, as people, all experience struggles. Some of those struggles are different, some are similar, and some may even be the same. Some of those struggles aren't difficult for one but could be detrimental to another. There is no differentiation between troubles a Christian experience and those of a non-Christian. The only difference is the manner in which we strive to handle the struggles.

Many situations that we consider struggles were actually steps to help us determine what we are passionate about. Those steps helped to guide us away from areas that were meant to harm us and would only kill the dream, the passion, and the destiny within. Other situations were steps designed to make and mold us for our destiny. They revealed to many of us what we can withstand, what we are really made of, what we are capable of. In essence, those situations revealed our possibilities.

Some of you may not have experienced struggle, but you have the question about destiny. How am I going to reach that part of my life? How can I obtain that goal? How do I obtain or reach them at this stage in my life? Is it too late for me? Have I somehow missed my time?

So, if you are reading this book and you're not a Christian, trust me, I understand what you are going through. I have been there, where I questioned what is it I was born to do and my ability to do what I feel I am meant to do? I believe my experience can help you avoid some of the pitfalls I had to endure, whether or not you're a Christian.

In this devotion, you are going to find women that look like you and me. Women who had a dream and a passion but did not know how it would come to fruition. They were running a race that had no destination, no determined end. They were all pregnant with purpose. There were a few who didn't recognize what they were pregnant with. Then there were others who aborted it because they didn't recognize they were pregnant. And then some miscarried or gave birth too soon.

These women, like you and I, had a determined end, a destiny, and they reached that destiny at all costs. As you journey through these pages, remember that you are not alone and you, too, have a determined end, a God-given destiny that you must reach. Take one step at a time and run the race that's laid before you. You may get tired, you may get weak, but you MUST keep going. "The race isn't given to the swift nor the strong but to the one that endures to the end." Go ahead, you can do it! I'll be right here with you every step of the way, and there are others waiting for you on the other side. See you at the finish line!!

TERMS TO KNOW

Before you go any further in this book, let me define a few terms to make you aware of the way they will be used in this text. If you will allow your mind to shift to understand these words as stated below and consider these definitions while reading.

PURPOSE

Considering one's purpose appears to be one of the most asked questions, "What is my purpose?" This question is asked not just on the spiritual level, but everyone wants to know or is curious about the meaning of their existence. Why am I here? Webster defines purpose by stating, "it is the reason something is done or used; the aim or intention of something." When I think of this definition, I think more of a motive for doing. For example, what is your heart's intention? So, I'd rather not use this definition in the text.

Another definition stated, "the feeling of being determined to do or achieve something, the aim or goal of a person." During this book, we will lean more towards this definition of purpose. And to go a little further, I would say we will look at purpose as the reason for which something exists or is made, an intended or desired result; end; aim; goal; determination. With this definition, there is movement; movement to become that in which you were created to be.

A cookie was created to be a cookie, regardless of what kind of cookie it is. It was created to be just that. There are many types of cookies. They are unique in their own right but still a cookie with the same purpose; to be eaten. In Ephesians 2:10, the apostle Paul says, "We are God's handiwork, created in Christ Jesus to do good works, which God prepared in advance for us to do." God calls you to a purpose — to do good works — "tailor-made" just for you.

PASSION

Passion is one of those words that people use often without really understanding the original meaning of the word. When most people refer to "passion", they use it to mean powerful emotions reflecting an intense desire or boundless enthusiasm for something, an obsession if you will. I think of passion as "that thing." That thing that will make you sick not to be able to do. That thing that burns within you, almost to the point of consumption, if you can't or don't do it. That thing that will lift your head in the most awful time. That thing that brings you joy even during times of sorrow. That thing that you dream of, whether it be daytime or times of slumber. That thing you feel you were put on this earth to do…. that thing!

That thing is your passion, your fire. Yet, many of us are grounded in time because of our fears, shortcomings, or our lack of self-confidence. Many of us are grounded from living out our destiny because of things that we have been told. We have poor self-esteem, and even though we desire it–we don't even believe that God can produce enough oxygen to get the fire burning hot enough to ignite and lift us, that business, that book, whatever that passion is, from the ground.

So, what is that subject, interest, or vision that stirs you up inside when you do it, think about it, or prepare for it? Whatever that is - when you connect that passion with an eternal perspective, you'll light a fire within.

Keep in mind that your purpose and your passion will always have eternity written in it if it is the destiny given to you by God. So, the question you need to ask yourself is this: What am I passionate about that has eternity connected to it?

Frequently in Scripture, it says that God "stirred" the heart of the person He was calling to do something. What has God stirred your heart to do? What brings out your emotions? What breaks your heart or inspires and invigorates you? What makes you feel alive when you do it, engage with it, or even think about it? If eternity is connected to it, that is your passion revealing your destiny. Go get it. Run after it. Pursue it. Chase it. Embrace it. Live it. Because without it, you won't be fulfilling your destiny, you will merely be existing.

The best question to ask regarding passion is, if it wasn't for money, family, or time–is there something in your life that you would do? What would that be? Do you have a secret ambition? If it is tied to eternity, then that is your passion. And unless you pursue your passion, you are going to die. I'm not talking about physical death, but what will happen is that you will die emotionally. Passion left unaddressed dies and takes a piece of your heart with it, or at the least - it remains squelched; suppressed.

ETERNITY

This one may seem obvious, but I want to make sure you fully understand what I'm saying to you. Eternity can be defined as unending time or endless life after death. When what you do is connected to eternity, the impact of it will live on, even after your death.

DESTINY

We have defined passion and eternity. Now I want to define destiny, as I will refer to it often during our time together. When I say destiny, I am speaking of God's preferred future for you. Our God determined destination; His determined or intended end. Not just His usage of you, but His usage of you at your maximum level of potential. The destiny I'm referring to is the thing that has been chosen for you before you were you. Come here Jeremiah... where God introduces him to his assignment. He says to this young prophet "before I formed you in your mother's womb, I knew you". In other words, He was saying you were born on purpose.

Psalm 37:23 tells us that "the steps of a good man are ordered by the Lord." Webster tells me that a step is an advance or movement made by raising the foot and bringing it down elsewhere. Another definition says a combination of foot or foot and body movements making up a unit or a repeated pattern. Therefore, steps are organized, steps are methodical and subsequent. The way we get the steps from God for His purpose, His destiny for our lives is through spending time with Him in prayer. It's during prayer that we learn His will and destiny for our lives. When we submit ourselves to God's will, He leads our decisions which organizes or orders our steps, we may not learn the big picture at that time or all of it at one time but the more time we spend with Him the more we learn. We learn what decisions to make to guide us to our destiny. Therefore, steps, biblically, are our decisions. Destiny is eternity. Destiny is what God has chosen for us. Our decisions are how we choose for ourselves what God has already chosen.

CHASE

Many hear the word chase and think of running away from something, and we have done that for far too long. We have run away from making the tough decisions when they didn't feel good. We have run away from the job that challenged us more than we were willing to be challenged. We have turned away from situations and things that may have pushed us into our divine place sooner. But I am here to help us be free.

When I say or use the word chase, it is the act of pursuing; to hurry after. It is the action that we will run or go after what we want. Run after that job, go after that dream, pursue that goal. It is the action that we will invoke; call on; seek earnestly. When I say chase, it will be the action we put forth to obtain what we were created to receive. When we are chasing destiny, we are earnestly seeking that in which we were created to do. After realizing that, we then pursue, run after it and continue until we have reached our pre-determined end. This happens when our will has become God's will and we are fulfilling whatever we were put on earth to pursue. Let's pray!

Prayer: Father God, you are awesome, and you are all-knowing. I come asking you to transform my thinking so that I may know what you want me to do. Saturate my soul with clear knowledge of your holy and perfect will for me. Reveal and confirm to me the passions connected with my eternal purpose. Light the fire within me that will propel me to do that which you have created me to do. Order my steps, Lord, as only you can, guide me, and allow each one of my steps to be an advancement for where you would have me to go, for where you would have me to work, to live. Lord, transform my mind that it may line up with your Word. Remove any negative thoughts and doubts. Allow my heart and mind to be opened to receive your will for my life, allow my will to become your will for me, allow my desires to become your desires that I may be transformed, and receive what Your Word has said concerning me. Lord, give me the strength and the endurance to run this race given to me to seek after, to chase after my determined end. In Jesus' name, Amen.

Scripture: Romans 12:1-2

PREPARATION FOR THE RACE

Throughout this devotional, you will encounter "Ponder & Pray" moments as well as "Ponder & Pace" moments. The purpose of these moments is to give yourself time for reflection, meditation, and participation or action. During these moments, you may choose to stop there and ponder for the rest of the day on what you read or do the action that was stated. You could also answer the questions and continue to the next section. These moments are intended to give you an opportunity to seek guidance from God. Sometimes we can be in such a hurry that we miss the moment or the revelation. The steps are intentionally there for pause, to give thought, and to listen to what your heart is saying. Take small pieces, read 15 minutes a day or pause for the cause at each action step.

Because this is a devotional that prompts actions to be taken, I don't want you to feel rushed. It is broken up into four weeks, however I didn't define the days. Take your time and be honest with yourself as you chase your destiny. No one else can do what you were purposed to do. Others may be purposed with similar assignments, but there is only one you and your journey is yours alone. Remember, the race isn't given to the swift nor the strong, but to the one that keeps running. Pause, Ponder, Pace and Pray as you run the race…

Week One

Hello! Hello! Are you talking to me? You can't possibly be talking to me. Do you know who I am? Do you know what I did? Do you know where I am from? You know I am not perfect, right? I don't always say or do the right things. You know I make mistakes, right? You can't be talking to me; I've done too much wrong, and some things I did are just downright embarrassing. If I think back, I am ashamed of them. Some things I did because I had to do what needed to be done. No, you can't possibly be talking to me. Hello? How about goodbye!! Because there is no way you are talking to me.

Many of us have these thoughts or have at some point; when we have been asked to do something that we don't think we are capable of doing. We second guess our abilities. Sometimes because of a lack of training, maybe poor self-esteem or possibly because of the things that we were told. Or better yet, the things we told ourselves. The things we have accepted that others said about us. The labels they put on us as well as the labels we put on ourselves. You know the things that labeled you or the things that mistakenly identified your value or your worth. The thing or things that resulted in the belief that we are not good enough for that job, that task, that position, that raise, that house, that car, that____ you fill in the blank.

We are overtaken by the guilt or the shame of the very things that make us qualified for the position or the call.

And because we are overtaken and do not see how sharing will help someone else avoid the pitfall, we fail to see that we are not alone and that there is life after that. Honestly, girl, it is that very thing you don't want anyone to know about that made your number come up on the list. So, go ahead, pick up the phone. Say hello! At least see who is calling.

> *Ponder & Pray*
> If you could spend the rest of your life doing or talking about one thing, what would it be?

I Am Called

Let me introduce you to a woman in the Bible that had a desire but thought she was too old to fulfill her desire. She not only ignored the phone, but she laughed at the caller on the other end. Check it out.

Sarah was married to Abraham, and the bible tells us she was childless because she could not conceive. The tension with the premise of the Abraham saga lies in the fact that God promised to make Abraham the founder of a mighty nation. Regarding the fulfillment of the promise, Sarah embodies the themes of fear and doubt. Her doubt drives Sarah to devise her own way of realizing the promise—she gives Abraham her maidservant, Hagar, so that Hagar might bear a child for them. When the promise is repeated, Sarah expresses her doubt in sarcastic laughter (Genesis 18:12).

This led Sarah to the logical conclusion that she would be the mother of many nations. This was the first call. His time wasn't her time, and it was so outrageous to her she laughed. God had given her the desire for a child and when it wasn't happening quickly enough, Sarah decided to do her own "thang," so to speak. She gave her handmaiden Hagar as her maternal stunt double. This act resulted in a child, but not the child that was promised to her or Abraham.

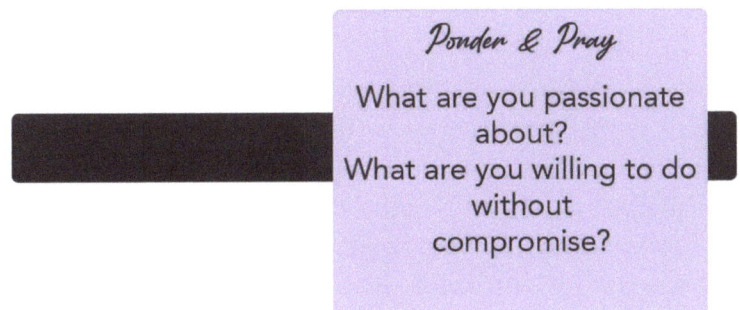

Ponder & Pray
What are you passionate about?
What are you willing to do without compromise?

WHAT IS THE CALL?

A call or calling can be defined as a strong inner impulse toward a particular course of action, especially when accompanied by a conviction of divine influence. Calling is the vocation or profession in which one customarily engages religiously. Those are the Webster definitions of the word, but many refer to the calling as a pull or a force that tugs you or directs you strongly toward something. They start as a tiny nagging thought or feeling, then begin to consume your mind and drive your everyday life. You'll feel a sense of urgency and a strong inclination to follow a calling, whereas a whim is often fleeting. The call may burn in you like a fire, like a passion.

HOW DO YOU KNOW THAT YOU ARE BEING CALLED?

For many people of faith, that question is alternately a source of mystery, frustration, confusion, and hope. Does God have a fine-tuned plan for each of us, or is God's call more general with the details left up to us? You'll likely find as many answers as the number of people that you ask.

God's first call began with the words "come here." The first call from Jesus began with "follow me." Following Jesus means we come to Him and learn who we are: sons and daughters of the king of the universe. But Jesus never stands still for long, and so our coming to Him always results in our following him. Before Jesus calls us to do, He first calls us to be; to simply be His. From that place of intimacy, where we are loved, known, and accepted.

But there is work that God calls all of us to do, and it's laid out for us in the Bible. God makes it clear again and again that we're to love others, care for the poor, and live our lives in such a way that we point to the power of the gospel. When we contemplate what God's calling is for our lives, those universal commands are a great place to start.

We are all called, and we are unique. We may have the same goals or passions but the way we go about them is different and because of that, your steps, your process, your path will be different from anyone else's. You have a unique contribution. There is someone on your path that needs what you possess. Therefore, it is so important that you get up and answer the call. It's not too late. You don't have to be perfect, you just have to be willing. You can answer even with your inadequacies; answer and God will guide you through the process. Answer the call, say hello!

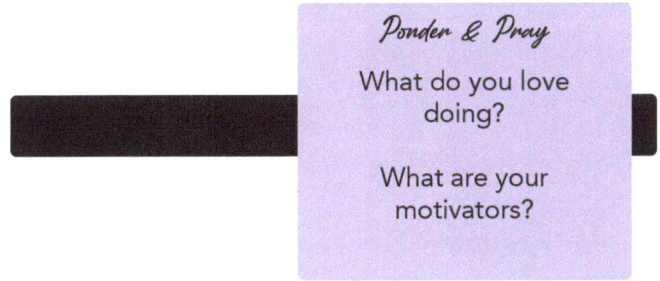

Ponder & Pray

What do you love doing?

What are your motivators?

WHAT IS GOD'S CALLING FOR YOUR LIFE?

It's a good thing God is not like our local telephone companies. His call is not a onetime event. His posture towards us is one of continual calling and invitation. The Christian is urged to "walk in a manner worthy of the calling to which you have been called" (Eph. 4:1) by living the "life that the Lord has assigned to him, and to which God has called him" (1 Cor. 7:17). In essence, God tells us, "This is who you are," and then he opens our eyes to how we should live in response to that call.

To put it another way, there's work to be done. God pronounced His creation "good" and then invited His children into the family business. He could've kept snapping his fingers and making new babies, gardens, and homes. Instead, He blessed His children with vocation. They make babies. They work the ground. They harvest food. They cultivate the world. Though God certainly works in supernatural ways, His work is more often of the regular variety. He feeds the world through farmers, funds business through bankers, and cultivates beauty through artists.

Yet calling gets more practical too. We are custom made by our Creator to fill a place and fulfill a destiny. We are summoned to serve a purpose. And arriving at that purpose requires us to answer certain questions that excavate our individuality. Ask yourself these questions:

> What are my talents? How am I gifted? What are my strengths and weaknesses? What comes easy to me? What am I naturally good at doing?

TALENTS

Talents are those things or areas that you excel in, such as cooking, graphic design, math, writing, singing, teaching, and many others. These things come with ease, extraordinarily little effort. Your talents allow you to be successful in work. Talents represent natural skills you already have or can develop with practice.

GIFTS

Gifts are special areas of life that God has blessed you with. Your gifts may include hospitality, administration, craftsmanship, discernment, evangelism, and more. Each of these gifts, and there are many more, are given to us by God. These gifts help us fulfill the calling that we have on our lives, our purpose. Therefore, our gifts are unique to each of us and where we are headed at that moment in our lives. Our experiences help to make these gifts unique as well.

As created beings, we are hard-wired with certain strengths and talents. These talents and gifts are not accidental. They speak to us of the path God invites us to travel, where we find jobs, roles, and service compatible with our giftings. It's like discovering the sport to which our equipment belongs. Exploring the question of endowment (which includes asking others) helps guide you toward your vocational call, your career, your employment.

What have I experienced?

The question of vocation meets us on a road already traveled. We aren't newborns. We arrive at adulthood having passed through significant experiences, struggles, and mishaps. A broken home, an unpleasant relationship, a nasty cousin that felt the need to take something that wasn't theirs to take, a college scholarship, a wayward sibling, an abusive parent, an uncle in rehab, and countless other milestones along our journey shape our calling. Our calling is vitally connected to our story. Understanding "who I am" and "how I got to be this way" are crucial questions in interpreting your experience and identifying my calling, my purpose, my destiny from God.

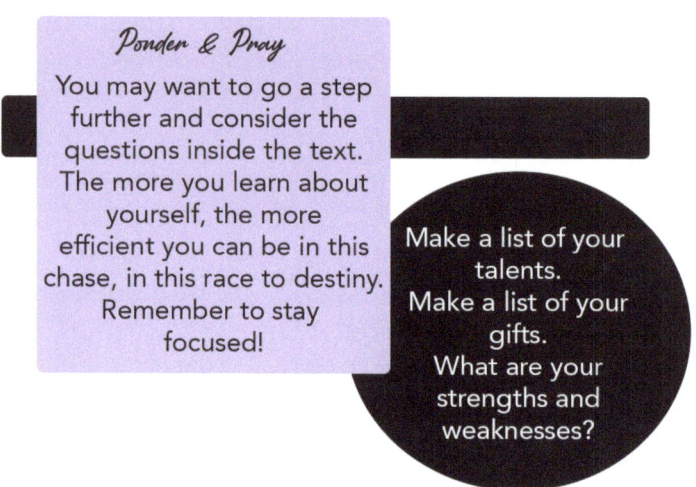

Ponder & Pray
You may want to go a step further and consider the questions inside the text. The more you learn about yourself, the more efficient you can be in this chase, in this race to destiny. Remember to stay focused!

Make a list of your talents.
Make a list of your gifts.
What are your strengths and weaknesses?

What do I enjoy?

We are not dispassionate, lifeless beings. We have passions, desires, aspirations—things we enjoy and feel irresistibly drawn to. They elicit pleasure from us, and when we're honest, we often feel God's pleasure in the pursuit. Vocation often follows passion and ambition. It's conceived when desire marries pursuit. It explores what makes us thrive. The question of enjoyment asks what pursuit brings us the greatest pleasure for the utmost glory of God. What makes you come alive? What would you do even if you didn't get paid to do it?

Before we continue identifying the call, remember that your call isn't permanent. Our calling may be fluid. God, in His ultimate design, allows us to experience different seasons of life. I know that throughout my life, I've been a single mother and married. I've lived in Florida and Virginia. I've worked full time, part time, been a mother as a full-time student, and been a stay-at-home mom. I've worshiped in COGIC, Baptist, and non-denominational churches. Each place, each season, is ordained by God. Each experience was a part of my destiny, it was part of my story. It is part of my steps that have been ordered. I haven't and still don't understand them all, but they have all been on my journey to destiny.

While it is fine to set goals and plan for the future, instead of worrying about tomorrow or next week, or next year, remember that God has you just where He wants you in this season of life. As you navigate this current season of life, be sure to place emphasis on faithfully serving Him where He's placed you until He makes it clear what His plan is for you. You may be saying, "but I am not spiritual." Then you work diligently where you are until you know that your next step has been established.

God may change your circumstances or your desires to guide you to another calling. Today's calling may not be tomorrow's calling from God. Our calling is an ongoing journey rather than a destination. Just as our lives are ever changing, as people we change as we grow and are refined. Our calling is the journey to destiny.

It's easy to look at your to-do list; the many loads of

laundry piling up, the taxes that need to be filed, the errands that need to be run, the meals that need to be prepped, and be overwhelmed – even questioning your calling and your purpose. I encourage you, however, to serve in these seemingly minor tasks with a glad heart. All will be revealed in time, even your call in each season of your life. What the future holds is not ours to determine. It is in Father God's hands. One of the key parts in the process of spiritual growth, however, is to pray for and identify our unique callings.

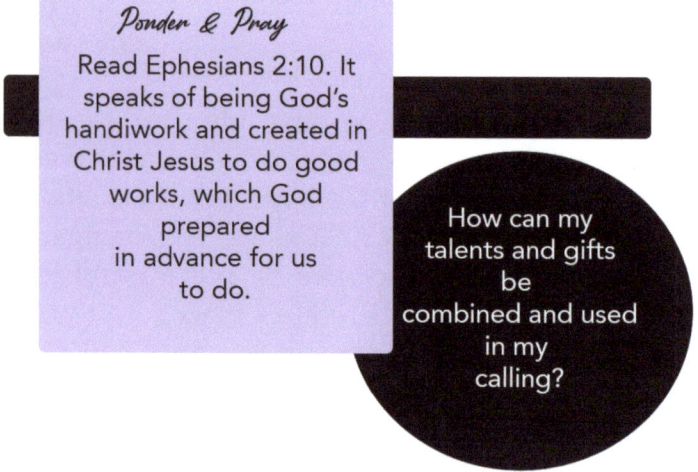

Ponder & Pray
Read Ephesians 2:10. It speaks of being God's handiwork and created in Christ Jesus to do good works, which God prepared in advance for us to do.

How can my talents and gifts be combined and used in my calling?

Now that we have discussed the call and what it may look like and may have even accepted that God can use us, we must now talk about training before operating in whatever it may be. When you get a job, you have experience or training before you go to work. Whether it was education or on-the-job training, training took place. We want to ensure that we are well equipped; we understand the correct way and how to do what we feel called to do so that we don't get hurt or hurt someone else.

KNOW WHO YOU ARE

Oprah Winfrey said, "Don't be confused between who people say you are and who you know you are." You are the one person you should know, undoubtedly. Webster tells us that knowing oneself is to understand one's own emotions, desires, and abilities. You should know what makes you happy and what upsets you. You should know if you hold back from sharing thoughts, emotions, or beliefs in relationships because of the fear of another's reactions. Are you aware of your emotions?

You are the expert of your being. You oversee your thoughts, and you own your personality. Independence and self-awareness are important to accepting the call. They are also linked to confidence. Knowing who you are and what you stand for in life can help to give you a strong sense of self-confidence.

Independence is about more than being able to take care of yourself. In this context, independence presents itself as the ability to love yourself. Self-awareness is a trait — or maybe "practice" is the more accurate way to put it — that everyone can always improve. It is part emotional intelligence, part perception, and part critical thinking. It means knowing your weaknesses, of course, but it also means knowing your strengths and what motivates you. It means knowing not only what makes you tick, but why something makes you tick. The combination of independence and self-awareness allow you to love yourself just as you are.

Let's take this a step further... who's the authentic you? Who is the REAL you? Authenticity means you are true to your own personality, values, and spirit, regardless of the pressure you're under to act otherwise. Authenticity happens when your words, actions, and behaviors consistently match your core identity. Again, being authentic starts with knowing who you are and being in touch with yourself in the moment.

Being you authentically means having a keen awareness of who you are and what you stand for, expressing yourself honestly and consistently to the world. Many of us may be one way with one group of people and another when around a different group. We are not being true to ourselves, nor the people around us. On a deeper level, authenticity illuminates the path forward to live the life you want. When you get clear on what matters to you, you make decisions that align with your identity and core values. You begin to build a life that brings you meaning and joy.

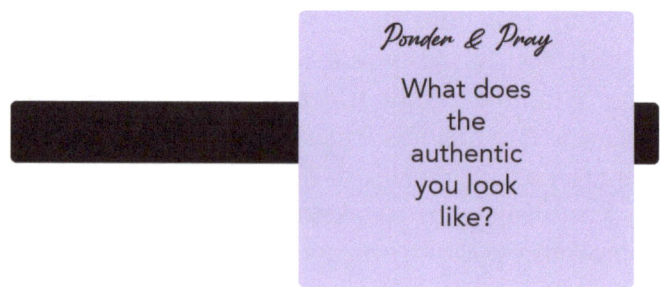

Ponder & Pray

What does the authentic you look like?

Being you authentically means speaking your opinions honestly in a healthy way, making decisions that align with your values and beliefs, pursuing your passions, listening to the inner voice guiding you forward, allowing yourself to be vulnerable and open-hearted but also setting boundaries and walking away from toxic situations.

However, remember to be kind and respectful. Authenticity doesn't mean expressing how you feel in a way that's hurtful or judgmental to others. Check in with yourself and learn the art of surrendering; everything doesn't have to be a fight and most of all it's not always your fight. Bring your complete self into everything you do and, most of all - trust yourself.

KNOW WHO YOU ARE IN HIM

Once you know who God is and rest in those truths, you will be changed. Especially after you learn, He isn't like man. He knows what we are going to do before we do it. He knows the mistakes we are going to make. He knows us better than we know ourselves. Embrace that and embrace the fact that He made you. When the Holy Spirit dwells in you, you will be closer to who God has created you to be. We are all his handiwork. We're all a work in progress but knowing Him is the first step.

The second step is to know what God says you are and who you are created to be. What attributes you are given?

You are chosen!
But you are a chosen people, a royal priesthood, a holy

nation, God's special possession, that you may declare the praises of him who called you out of darkness into his wonderful light. — 1 Peter 2:9

You are loved!
How priceless is your unfailing love, O God! People take refuge in the shadow of your wings. — Psalm 36:7

You are redeemed!
In him, we have redemption through his blood, the forgiveness of sins, in accordance with the riches of God's grace — Ephesians 1:7.

You are beautiful!
You are altogether beautiful, my darling; there is no flaw in you. — Song of Songs 4:7

You are His!
Yet to all who did receive him, to those who believed in his name, he gave the right to become children of God — John 1:12

Your calling will use your talents and gifts, uniquely bestowed on you by God, but you must know who He created you to be in order to fulfill your purpose on this earth. It is my prayer that you will acknowledge and accept the call and run the race that is put before you.

Perhaps you are living in a Sarah season. Right now, you don't believe; you don't see yourself doing that____ (you fill in the blank). Perhaps you are struggling with disappointment over a dream denied, or a promise postponed. Maybe you feel like it's too late for you to start, but it is not. You never know when you'll give birth to a promise. I want to encourage you today to answer the call. You don't have to be perfect; you will make mistakes along the way, but remember the call is on the journey to destiny. Chase Destiny!!

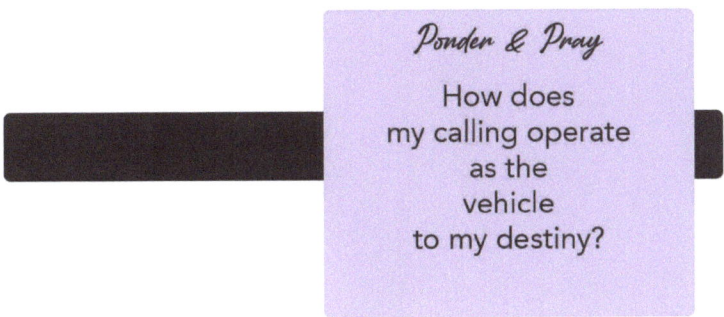

Ponder & Pray

How does my calling operate as the vehicle to my destiny?

PRAYER:

Lord, help me to embrace your calling for my life with equal parts fervor, wisdom, and humility as I surrender my life and everything in it to you. I know you've blessed me with unique talents and gifts. Help me understand how to nurture and use these gifts and talents to bring glory to You. Even on my daily journey, my job, my career, and my education allow those gifts and talents to glorify you. Allow me to see and understand that the gifts and talents aren't for me but tools to use on my journey to destiny.

Bless my choices in every area of my life, vocation, and ministry. Transform the desires of my heart and purify them so that they are pleasing to you. Help me to see through Your eyes and love others as You love us. No matter what I face each day, Lord, allow me to hear Your call and seek You always. Amen.

Scripture: 1 Peter 4:10-11

Week Two

As you sit and look at yourself in the mirror, many questions go through your mind. After realizing what your talents are and your strengths and weaknesses, you now have another set of questions. Did I just hear what I think I heard? Where do I begin? What does that consist of? What training do I need? Is there training involved? How will I get help? Is it possible to find a mentor for this? What if I mess up? I can't do that. They make that look so easy. No, I can't believe that I am expected to do that. I have always been told that I am not good enough or that I am not smart enough. I don't speak well. People don't like me; I didn't have many friends growing up. How do I accomplish this task? I want to continue; I want to do it, but am I capable? Do I trust what I heard?

> **Ponder & Pray**
>
> Set aside an alloted time to spend seeking God's face each day. Write down any new revelations you have received this week.

Believing the Call

When we are kids, some of us had dreams or ideas of

what we wanted to do when we grew up. We knew what job or career we wanted, whether we wanted to be married or not, and approximately how many children we wanted, if any at all. These goals did not come without planning. We investigated how much money we would make. We researched what training was needed for that career. We made plans to do well in school and to obtain the credentials needed to reach the goal. We may have run into some snags along the way, but we found what adjustments needed to be made and we made them and continued.

Then some may not have done well in school or decided that college wasn't their path, so they decided what they wanted to do to make a living. For some, it may have been formal, such as secondary education or a degree. For others, it may have been hands-on, such as on-the-job training, military, or Job Corps. Finally, some may have gone through some sort of vocational training. Even if by chance you were given a business or job; training was still a part of your success. Preparation was put into that goal, that dream, that career. The same preparation that happens for a secular job should happen in the spiritual, for your call, your purpose.

Let me introduce you to a woman that was abandoned, oppressed, lonely, and tossed around by the world. However, she was also beautiful, strong, bold, and faithful. She suffered the loss of her parents, which would have been painful and maybe even left her feeling alone. She was a foreigner in a land that wasn't her home. Therefore, she may have felt displaced. Nonetheless, she didn't let these obstacles prevent her from answering, believing, and preparing for the call.

Esther is an orphan, being cared for by her cousin Mordecai, a Jewish official in the royal court. Esther is a young girl of marriageable age and is selected as one of the empire's beauties, to be considered by the king as a possible queen. Esther was chosen and placed in the royal women's quarter to undergo a year of training and beauty treatments. She spent a year being taught how to sit, walk and talk. She learned what the king does and does not like; how and when to respond. A year of studying how to dance, what attitude to carry, what persona to give off, when to look away and when to make eye contact. She studied her craft, her call, her job; she knew what was expected of her as a queen.

Even after Esther was selected to be queen, she maintained contact with Mordecai and sought his advice. Due to Mordecai's bidding, she had kept the fact that she was Jewish a secret. When Mordecai uncovered the plot to kill him and all the Jews, he reminded her she would be killed as well. He asked her to ensure the king was aware of this plot because it was unlike the king to order a slaughter. Again, this took preparation because it wasn't customary for the queen to go into the king unless he sent for her. As a matter of fact, it was against the law. Esther was afraid because the king hadn't called for her in a month and she knew going in uninvited could greatly offend the king and lead to her death.

After a few days, she asked Mordecai to tell all Jews to fast for the next three days. She didn't just go into the king; she recalled her training; she prepared herself through prayer and fasting. Esther had decided "…If I perish, I perish" (Est 4:16). Esther remembered her people, and she was willing to sacrifice her life to save them. In the end, Esther found in her faith the courage to approach the king and appeal to him. She was successful in her appeal and the king ordered the death of the man responsible for the plot on the Jews' life.

> *Ponder & Pray*
>
> Go to www.onetcenter.org/tools
>
> What did you learn about yourself from the assessment?

Where Do I Begin?

Whenever we are curious about something or want to know something, we research. Now you know you are "Detective Diva" so don't act like this is any different. After you have identified, pondered, and prayed, now it's time to collect as much knowledge as you can about what you are called to do, your dream, your goal. You are going to collect information from various sources. You're going to find out what the task consists of. Not only what you need to do the task, but what do you need to have? Is there a mentorship involved? Does it involve working with people? Am I good at working with people? Am I working with adults, children, the elderly, or all the above? What must be done for preparation?

Gathering information about the task is great and let's not forget about the internal preparation you need. What is the condition of my heart? Am I hurting in some area of my life that may affect the task? Do I need mental healing? Can I be nicer? Am I approachable? What is my attitude? What type of emotional preparation do you, as a person, need to be ready for the training that is needed for the call, the dream, the goal?

Esther wasn't only prepared physically, but she was trained in her obedience and her response to the call. Esther was taught what it meant to be the Queen. She learned her responsibilities and how to respond to them. She learned what the King liked and how important it was to please the King. She didn't just wake up and decide she was ready to be Queen after she was called to the position, but she was prepared for the weight of the responsibilities that came with that title. There is preparation before operation!!

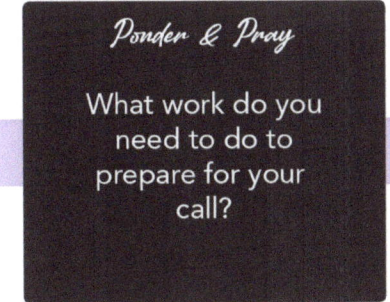

Ponder & Pray

What work do you need to do to prepare for your call?

Let The Preparation Begin...

There are various ways and types of research. How you go about that research depends on how in-depth you desire to go before applying what you've learned or just how much you need to know about your dream, your goal, and your call. This is the time you find out everything you can about what you are about to embark on. You are moving forward toward destiny, and you want to be ready.

> **Ponder & Pray**
>
> Is there some type of education/professional development/certificate that will help prepare you for the call?

RESEARCH METHODS

There are many ways to get information. The most common research methods are books, YouTube, Google, personal interviews, courses, Podcasts, websites, talking with people, and the list goes on. The bottom line is there is much information to be gathered to learn more. The better prepared you are, the more confident you will find yourself.

My personal journey included adding the bible to my research. I wanted to know what God had to say about the call that was on my life. I also wanted to know how people in the bible did what He had called me to do. I read and studied not only what the call consists of, but what was the attitude of the people, what was their body language, how did they have to carry themselves? What was the cost of doing the task placed before me?

Internet

With the help of the internet, we can easily find the information we need, without spending endless hours. This is where you can get a general understanding of what it is you are looking for. You can find the type of training that will be needed as well as when and where to begin that training. Don't rely exclusively on internet resources. The internet is general and remember anyone can post on the web, so double-check the source by looking up your call, your dream, your goal using another method as well.

Literature Searches

A literature search is a search of all types of literature, such; as books and peer-reviewed articles on your topic. A literature search provides not only an opportunity to learn more about a given topic, but it provides insight into how the topic was studied by others. It helps to interpret ideas, detect shortcomings, and recognize opportunities. It will help you to not make some of the same mistakes that were made previously. Reading a good book on the call, the dream job, or the goal that you have set out for yourself allows you to realize what you need.

Talking with People

Communication is going to be key during this part of the process. You will spend time talking with people who are knowledgeable about what you want to achieve. You are going to interview them and ask every question you can think of. Look to identify experts and, while talking with them, consider the possibility of them becoming a mentor. Yes, I know everyone's story is different, but they should be able to share their experience as well as their pathway of gaining knowledge in the area of interest. If they are currently in that area, you may ask to watch them so you can get a better understanding to go with your research up to this point.

Other Resources

There may be a course that you can take to better prepare you. Take a class in person or through an online platform. During this course, you will be equipped to complete the task given. This course may not be a degree course, but it is preparation all the same. Watch YouTube videos on your call. You may even listen to Podcasts. Either way, you are preparing for the race.

SELF EVALUATION

This is going to be the best part of this process. You have collected information on the call, the dream, the goal. You have done the research now let's begin the "me-search." What is already inside of you? What are your strengths and weaknesses? This is the time you have a few hard conversations with people you trust so they can reveal what you don't see. They can identify the weaknesses you have yet to realize or don't think exist. Those people will also be able to point out the strengths that come easily to you, so you don't recognize them as strengths. This isn't meant to be a "beat you up" conversation, but an honest conversation to help you become the best version of yourself possible.

During this self-evaluation, you are to ensure that you are healthy, not just physically, but mentally and emotionally. Emotional healing is the ability to acknowledge events and circumstances in our lives that may hinder us from moving forward. It's a process that allows us to take control of our thoughts, feelings, and emotions. Being healed emotionally will allow you to become aware and capable of exploring your feelings to deepen your self-awareness. This awareness will teach you to set boundaries in areas that are needed.

> *Ponder & Pray*
>
> Ask your friends to share what they believe to be your strengths and weaknesses.
>
> Is there someone who could serve as a mentor to you?

Remember, be the authentic YOU!! The authentic you get to live according to your own values and goals, rather than those of other people. Be true to your own personality, values, and spirit, regardless of the pressure that you're under to act otherwise. However, take into consideration the information that you learned about yourself. Use that information to evaluate whether or not the perception you are releasing is the image you want others to see. Are your values and goals being perceived in the manner in which you would like and intend to be received? Use what you learn about yourself to help push you into your destined place.

SEEK GOD'S FACE

In my life, fulfilling my destiny–my predetermined end is important to me. Again, it is my opinion that all of us were birthed, brought into this world, placed in our mother's womb with a purpose in mind. Our parents had to come together to be our parents. Whether we feel that was good or bad, it had to happen; it was for a purpose. The things, the trials, and tribulations, the situations we encountered, positive and negative, were all steps in the process of fulfilling our determined end. They were steps in the process of creating us to be who God has purposed us to be when He created us in our mother's womb. Therefore, as a part of my research, I spend time in prayer, meditating, and reading the Bible.

During this time, I am seeking answers to the many questions I have, things I don't understand but also direction; direction in this plan that He has for me; direction and instruction in this life He has purposed for me. I have come to know myself during my "me-search" and evaluation. I'm not always levelheaded in my thinking. I'm not always calm, so I spend time asking Him to help me be more understanding and to obtain more of the attributes that I didn't and sometimes still do not have that I found was needed during my research phase. I spend time reading the bible and other materials as it is brought to my attention the attribute, talent, or anything that is needed to complete the task that the call, the dream, the goal requires of me. I spend time in prayer and reading on how to obtain and possess the necessary attributes needed to become a better version of myself. I need to be able to meet the prerequisites, the steps that are needed for my training to be complete in this area, in this season of my life.

It Is Personal

Some of you may be wondering what this looks like. First, any spiritual relationship is personal, and each one is just as unique as we are. The way you talk to your God may not be how I speak with my God. But for those of you that are interested in what this looks like, I will allow you to look in on my ritual. This changes sometimes depending on the season of my life that I am in. That means it changes when I am seeking answers versus when I am just loving and appreciating Him.

When I first begin, I make sure that I have a pencil and paper with me. I am expecting an answer, so I am prepared to take notes or write down what I feel He says to me, whether that is through scripture that is laid on my heart to turn to, or a sense of peace that is given to me. I don't always receive an answer the first, second, or the third time, but I get strength and peace in the midst of the transformation that is taking place in my life that is ultimately leading me to my destiny.

After I have pencil and paper, I find a nice quiet place that I can be aware or attentive to what I am expecting. I am away from any distractions that may cause me to miss the feeling of peace or direction. While in that place, I begin to play music, worship music to usher in the Holy Spirit, or invite God's presence in. As I begin, I worship and thank Him. I love Him for being who He is in my life, for being what I need, and for always being there for me.

Then I move into my petition, asking for what I need, or expressing my confusion or my hurt in what I am going through or where I am in my life. Then I ask him for clarity on how it is to help me and what am I to take from this lesson. Was I wrong in something I did? What is my next step? By now in my time with God, I am usually walking back and forth, pacing. Whatever I am feeling in the moment, I express during this time. At the end of this, usually, I am laid on the floor, in tears, but waiting.

Waiting!?! Yes, I am waiting for my next step. I am waiting for my next set of instructions. I am waiting for Him to tell me where I went wrong or if I went wrong. I am waiting for His guidance because He is the only one that knows how this story called my life ends. When I seek His face, I feel strengthened even before I get an answer. I realize that the weight of my concern has been lifted from me, so I am strengthened to continue or to stand until the next instruction is given. Again, I don't always get an answer or instructions at that time, so in those times I have to stand on the last instruction given and just wait. Sometimes it feels uncomfortable to wait in a place of the unknown or in a place where you don't know the next step. It is uncomfortable to stand when you are standing in a place where there is hurt. Just know that you can continue to go to God, and He is always there.

It is important to set aside time to spend with God to be able to seek His face for instructions, direction, and steps to take in your life. It is equally important to take time to stop and listen. You can't go in doing all the talking and then never wait for a response. During this time, you are groomed into who you need to be for what He has concerning you. You have to be sensitive enough to the spirit to be able to hear, see or notice a response even when you aren't in your prayer time. Something may happen throughout the day, and He uses that experience to answer your prayer. Be intentional and be aware.

> *Ponder & Pray*
>
> Is what you are called
> to do
> lining up with what you
> found out about
> this week?

This is real now!!! After a week of revelation, conversation, and consideration, the time has now come for you to do the work. Queen, you are like Esther when Mordecai came to her to remind her who she was that she was born a Jew. I am here to remind you that you, too, were born for a purpose. No doubt Esther didn't come into the king's presence offering a list of excuses. Don't make the mistake of responding to the call by who you're not and what you can't do.

Today, I call you "queen." You may not feel like a queen; you may not look like a queen; you may feel like you don't deserve to be a queen, but the scepter is still extended to you. I encourage you to go through the training. It may take a year or more but remember the call is on the journey to destiny!! Chase Destiny, Queen!!

> **Ponder & Pray**
>
> Did you learn anything new?
>
> Does what you learned about yourself line up with your call? How?

PRAYER:

Dear Heavenly Father, you are the Creator of all things, and You sustain all life. I come to you, acknowledging that your will is best and that your plan is far greater than any I could ever ask for or imagine. You said that without faith; it is impossible to please you. But whoever would draw near to you, God, must believe that you exist, and you reward those who seek you. I come seeking you for direction for who you have called me to be. I come asking you to order my steps. Bless my hands as you lead me where you've predestined me to go and to do. Give clarity where there may be confusion on what I am to do, where to begin or whom to talk with. Give me an ear to listen and a heart to receive. Open my mind and heart to all that I need to pursue.

God show me myself, cross-examine me, test my motives and affections. Show me areas that need healing, areas that need to be cut away, areas that will hinder me as I wait patiently, and listen for anything you reveal to me. Create in me a clean heart and renew in me a right spirit. Now your Word says all I need is faith the size of a mustard seed and I am holding on to that today. I am believing what you said concerning me, my dream, my goal, and my call. I will stand on that word. Your word also says that faith is confidence in what we hope for and assurance about what we do not see. Even though I may not see the manifestation, the evidence of who you say that I am, I am standing on that word confidently.

Thank you for being a God who loves me in spite of me. Thank you for trusting me and believing in me when I don't believe in myself. Thank you for everything and I seal this prayer in Jesus' name. Amen.

Scripture: Matthew 21:22

Week Three

What is hindering you or holding you back at this point from moving forward in your dream, your goal, your call in this season of your life? Could it be self-doubt, self-esteem issues, fear of what people will say, or wanting to be accepted? What is it that has you stagnant? You've done the research and have learned what it will take for you to accomplish the task. You've learned your strengths and weaknesses. You've had deep conversations or the hard talks with people you can trust to share some unseen strengths and weaknesses–so what are you waiting on?

Revealing The Call

Let's look briefly at two women that used fear to thrust them into their purpose. However, we could say that their fear was more of reverence than being frightened or afraid. Instead of allowing fear to control them, they allowed fear to push them. Nonetheless, their passion propelled them into their calling that inspired change. Because they didn't allow fear to hinder them, they changed the lives of many people.

Puah and Shiphrah were Hebrew midwives that we will find in the first chapter of Exodus. As the Israelites in Egypt began to proliferate or increase in numbers following the death of Joseph, Pharaoh, the king, sought to curb the Israelite's population. He was afraid that if war were to erupt, he and his army would be outnumbered by the Israelites, and they could lose. Therefore, Pharaoh commanded the Hebrew midwives, which only two are known by name, to kill all the Hebrew males at birth, but permit the females to live. However, Puah and Shiphrah didn't do as Pharaoh commanded. Instead, they saved the lives of the Hebrew baby boys by telling Pharaoh the births were finished by the time they arrived. They feared God more than they feared Pharaoh.

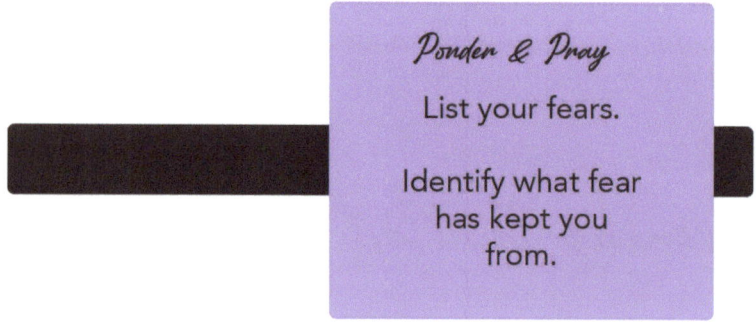

Ponder & Pray

List your fears.

Identify what fear has kept you from.

These two women could have been killed for not doing what they were ordered to do, but they didn't allow the fear of their lives being taken away to prevent them from saving the lives of the males that were born. Among those males was Moses, and because his life was spared, history was changed. These two midwives inspired change for many generations. How can you use your fear to push you into your destiny?

F.E.A.R.

"Courage is not simply one of the virtues, but the form of every virtue at the testing point." C. S. Lewis

Is it possible that fear is the culprit, the chains that have you bound? Webster defines fear as an unpleasant, often strong emotion caused by anticipation or awareness of danger or threat, a feeling of anxiety. Let's deal with the first part of this definition, "a strong emotion caused by anticipation or awareness of danger." Is there a portion of or any part of your dream, goals, or call putting you in danger? Let's dissect this so that we can kill it. Will you or anyone be placed in danger if you move forward? Think long and hard before answering that question. If your answer is yes, then fear may be warranted. But if your answer is no, then your fear is unwarranted.

I know you are saying fear is real, and it exists, and yes, it does. I, myself, deal with fear, but when it was broken down to me in this way, it made me look deeper into what was holding me back, what was hindering me; what truly had me bound. So, bear with me, don't throw in the towel just yet!

Researchers show that fear is a natural, powerful, and primitive human emotion. It involves biochemical responses as well as high individual emotional responses. Fear alerts the presence of danger or the threat of harm, whether it is physical or psychological. Sometimes fear stems from real threats, but it can also originate from imagined dangers. Because you have come to the understanding that the dream, the goal, the call isn't placing you in harm's way physically because there is no physical danger, let's go with the psychological, the imagined threat. The emotional response to fear is highly personalized; it is your own.

Fear involves some of the same chemical reactions in our brain as positive emotions, such as happiness and excitement and the things you deem fun and exhilarating. Some fears may be a result of experiences of trauma, while others may represent a loss of control. Nonetheless, we are discussing these fears to recall or evoke what is holding you back. What experience in your past or traumatic experience has you fearful of moving forward? What did you lose control over in the past that causes you to see your dream, your goal, your call similar to your past experience? Now if you recall in the previous weeks, we discussed your call is a portion of your experience–they are not to stagnate you but orchestrated to equip you.

If you're bound by past trauma or experience that prevents movement forward, then you may want to take a moment to think and ask yourself, are you healed? Are you healed emotionally and mentally from that situation? If your answer is no, that's okay, but healing needs to take place. That doesn't mean you can't do what you are called to do or that you need not pursue your dream. It means you need to identify and work on getting healed in that area so that it doesn't hinder you. Our past shapes us and helps us identify who we are and where we are headed.

Do I Need Healing?

Some of you may be struggling with letting go of the

fear, pain, or regret, or may be asking how to do that. Healing from past pain, fears, and traumatic experiences is not something that happens overnight. It is a process that requires patience, dedication, and commitment to change. It takes work. We, as humans, are wired to want to feel good and to minimize feeling bad, which often triggers self-sabotaging behavior in an attempt to avoid the pain. When we experience a painful event, it can rewire us for self-preservation. We then live in a "fight or flight" mode, constantly anticipating more pain in our lives, which is unconsciously welcomed through our actions. Therefore, we find ourselves going in a cycle. However, by consciously being present and aware when similar situations occur and making a different choice, you create a new outcome and an opportunity to create a different emotional response that may take you out of the "fight or flight" mode. This gives a positive emotional experience to the one that the brain had hardwired negative. Easily said… "a reset."

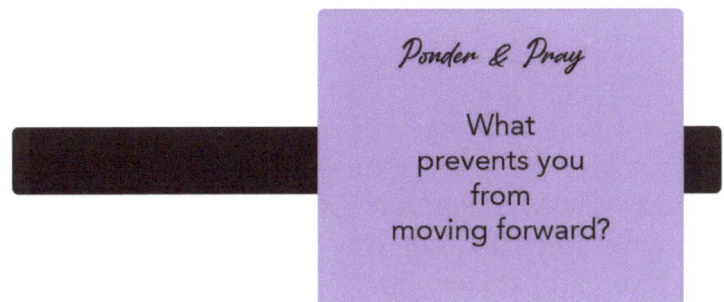

Ponder & Pray

What prevents you from moving forward?

Reset simply means to set again, anew. About "fight or flight" mode, you will envision the outcome you want or would like to have. Determine your core values or how it relates to your core values and set clear goals for what you want to accomplish. Break your goals into actionable steps and do them. Create the positive results you would have preferred. This new action will then be rewired, and it will help your emotional response in the future as you begin to do the action, and because the reaction was positive, there is no need for "fight or flight" mode in those situations.

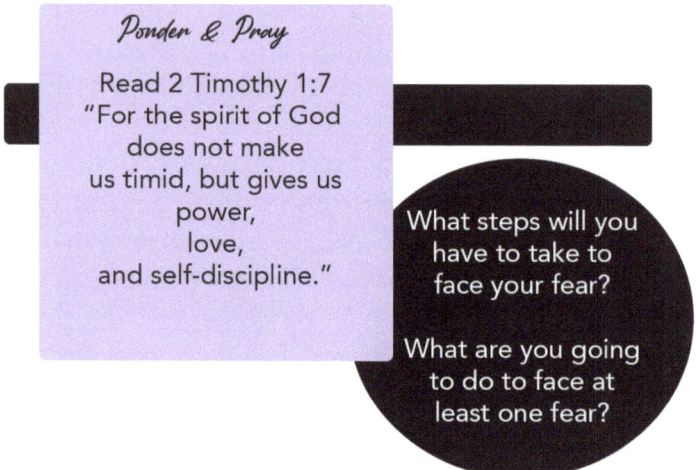

Ponder & Pray

Read 2 Timothy 1:7
"For the spirit of God does not make us timid, but gives us power, love, and self-discipline."

What steps will you have to take to face your fear?

What are you going to do to face at least one fear?

In the past, you may have experienced a situation and were unable to communicate your feelings. For whatever reason, if you don't get that opportunity, you can remain stuck in that place emotionally, so when things look similar, or situations look or feel familiar, you react to it because of the lack of expression in the past. You may not have expressed it or communicated how you felt. Or you may have, but the fear of feeling the same way and losing control haunts you. However, you don't have to stay there; you don't have to stay stuck. You can release by allowing yourself to express your emotions and communicate your feelings with someone you trust.

Honestly, seeking professional help isn't a bad idea. Many may have internalized some things that were not theirs to hold on to. Some may not have had the best childhood and need to be able to discuss those things and how they play a part in who I have become. Some of us need counseling to help us find our triggers, deal with our past, and to help us to be healthy enough to be able to complete the call, the dream, the purpose, the goals. If that is your reality, own it. If that is your fear, own it; own it and use it to move forward.

WALK IT OUT

Walk it out? You may be asking, what does that look like? Exactly what does it mean to walk it out? Walk it out means to conquer your fear. Look at what you are afraid of and tell it to move out of your way. Say to it, "I am moving forward at all costs." I acknowledge that you are there, but I am pushing, I am pressing toward the mark and that mark is my destiny, my dream, my goal. I may stumble along the way, but I am moving forward. I may make some mistakes, but I won't allow those mistakes to hinder me, stop me, or derail me!

For someone, "walk it out" may be as simple as telling a friend what you are doing and asking them to hold you accountable to what you said. For another one, it may be calling yourself what you are striving for… I am an entrepreneur, I am a baker, I am an author. You may finally be acknowledging out loud who you are called to be in this season of your life, in this step of the process, in this area of the journey.

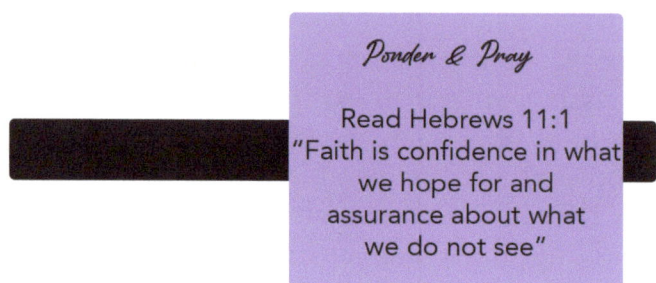

Your steps don't have to be huge; small steps will do. Just take the step! For the business owner, you may make business cards, create a flyer, or give out samples. Another may sign up for a class, begin listening to a podcast, or reach out to that mentor. But each step moves you toward the mark. Whatever it may be, do it!

You may be reading this and say, "Okay, I can do any of those things." Or you may be someone who says, "How do I walk in it when my calling in this season may be spiritual? What do I do?" My answer to you is simple. Walk by faith and not by sight. You must have faith. It is imperative that you trust and obey. Human nature causes us to want to control as much of our life and circumstances as we can. But following our calling requires us to learn to trust and obey God. Just as parents have their children's best interest at heart, so does God. Children learn to trust and obey their parents as they recognize their intentions are good. The only way to know this is to know God. That means spending time reading the bible, asking for understanding as you read, and talking with Him but listening as well. And like parents, you will be given instructions that may not be repeated, so listen and write them down.

As we receive the instructions, we must be patient because timing is important as well. I'm an impatient person by nature. I like immediate results. Just ask my husband. When I ask him to do something for me, I want him to do it right then, not an hour later, not tomorrow. Following my calling has taught me to wait on God, to trust His timing, and to not try to force my schedule. I must humble myself to patiently wait, to trust God's judgment, not my own, and to walk in obedience to God. Psalm 46:10 is a constant reminder for me to "Be still and know that I am God," to slow down, wait, and listen.

Walking it out also consists of asking for help. Children cry out to their parents when they need help. Similarly, as Christians, we can cry out for help and God will answer our prayers. There have been times when I was at a loss and facing a mountain that I couldn't move. God doesn't expect nor does He want us to face challenges alone. He wants us to ask Him for help. He will instruct you or tell you whom or what resource to use for help.

We aren't made to walk it out alone, but we must take the first step. Remember, a step is an act or movement of putting one leg in front of the other. When we take steps, we move. We are not standing in one place. When we take steps, we plan, we advance, we develop, we move forward. Walk it out, Queen! Walk it out!

STAY FOCUSED

In anything that we have planned out, we must stay focused. It's so easy to get distracted these days with the internet, iPhones, and social media. Once I know where God wants me to focus my time, I attempt to stay laser focused. I prioritize my time better, eliminate time wasters, and spend my precious time focused on what is most important. Another type of distraction is when people question your motive for helping someone or your motive for what you are doing. This has happened to me in the past. I remember being surprised and hurt when I learned someone was questioning why I was helping someone I barely knew. It didn't make sense to them, so they questioned me and, for a moment, caused me to question myself. Now, I have learned not to let this distract me from following my spiritual calling. The work I am doing is too important to God's plan. Everyone will not understand, nor can they see what is placed in front of me, so I have learned not to allow those to become distractions.

BE A TEAM PLAYER

We must be team players. We are part of a body. Our body has limbs and organs that allow our bodies to function properly. We all like pats on the back, and while I don't like to be center stage, I won't lie and say I don't like compliments. However, God has taught me that my role in His plan can be small or big because ultimately, it's not about me, it's about fulfilling His plan. And even if my role is tiny, I need to fulfill it, to be a team player.

Now, to do any of these things, we must make ourselves available. We tend to turn down opportunities to follow our calling when we think we are "too busy" with other things. We must be ready and willing to do what God calls us to do; otherwise, we miss an opportunity and sometimes we miss a need greater than our own. It's all about bringing glory to God, not ourselves. These opportunities usually groom us, and we miss them because we aren't making ourselves available. God isn't interested in impressive human talent and natural ability. He's looking for humble people who are totally dependent upon Him and willing to make themselves available for whatever He calls them to do. If you'll simply depend on Christ, make yourself available, and obey Him, He'll use you for His glory.

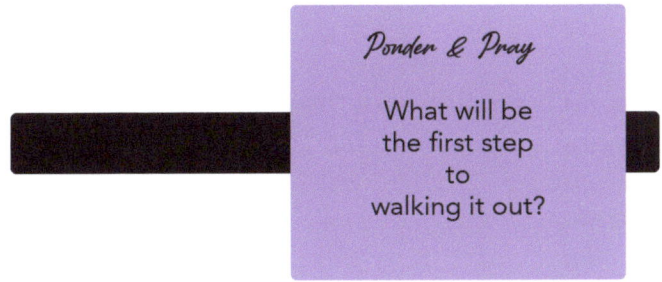

Ponder & Pray

What will be the first step to walking it out?

FACE YOUR FEARS

Following my spiritual calling has required me to face my fears. I am by nature a planner, so I like to know what's ahead of me before I dive in. I know I have missed God's best because apprehension has kept me from stepping out in faith to do His will. Recently, I found myself stuck, paralyzed by fear-fear of the overwhelming situation standing in front of me, fear of diving in and fear of finding no end in sight, fear of giving up so much of my time for an indefinite period. Sometimes you have to walk it out, afraid. Yes, following our calling can be scary, but it is also rewarding.

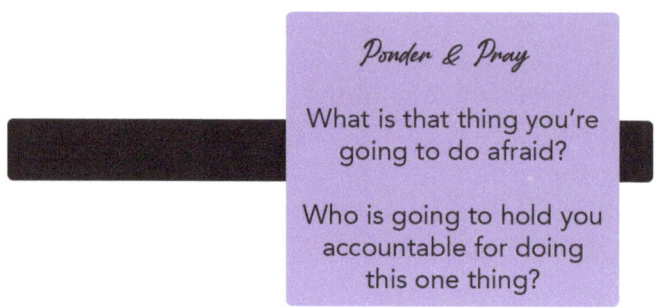

Ponder & Pray

What is that thing you're going to do afraid?

Who is going to hold you accountable for doing this one thing?

We must get the mindset of the Hebrew midwives, Puah and Shiphrah. They were fearful, but they allowed that fear to move them into their destiny, their predetermined end. They didn't allow the idea that Pharaoh could order them killed; they didn't allow what others may say; they didn't allow themselves to hinder them nor stop them. They didn't give fear power over them. They moved forward at all costs, their movement opened the door for Moses and freedom. Take hold of your freedom, release fear and walk into your destiny!!

PRAYER:

Lord, you are my light, and my salvation. Why should I be afraid? But sometimes I am! Protect me from danger. Give me confidence in you. You know that we live in a crazy and chaotic world. You also know my struggles in my daily life. When life gets to be too much, please calm my thoughts and emotions, and open my heart to your peace, comfort, and wisdom. Remind me I am encouraged by your word that says you have given me a spirit of power, love, and self-discipline, and not a spirit of fear and timidity. I pray your words will grow within my spirit and make me strong enough to do your will.

God, give me confidence in you so that I am sure of what you want from and for me, that I may walk boldly in the things you have for me. That I may bear the fruit that you desire as I walk out the plan that you have predestined for me. God, give me wisdom that my desires, my goal, and my will line up with what you have placed in me to fulfill in the way you desire. I thank you for answering my prayer. In Jesus' name. Amen.

Scripture: 2 Timothy 1:7

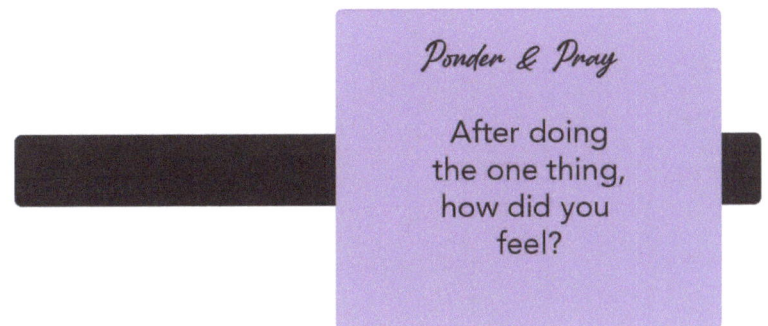

Ponder & Pray

After doing the one thing, how did you feel?

Week Four

Congratulations!!! You have made it to the race!!! The chase is on... you have heard and answered the call; you have accepted, acknowledged, and believed what was said. You have done the research, the work, and prepared for the task at hand. You have received direction and instructions; you have stood in the face of your fears; you are standing here at the starting line, bold and ready to pursue.

My sister, beautiful Queen, you are standing at the starting line ready to run after that job, go after that dream, that goal. You are ready to chase destiny, to earnestly seek that in which you were created to do. You are ready to run after it and continue until you have reached your pre-determined end. Remember, there will be obstacles, there will be setbacks, there will be strained muscles, there will be hurdles to jump and there will be hills to climb, but you are not alone. See you at the finish line!!

Chase Destiny

Before we plunge into the last leg of this race, I would like you to review the life of a strong woman that life was changed by a decision to chase her destiny. She may not have known at the time, but the decision she was about to make would change her and her family's life forever. She may have known that her life would change, but to what extinct. She didn't ponder on the results or consequences so much as the opportunity to maximize the moment. She was going to use all she had placed in her hands at this moment.

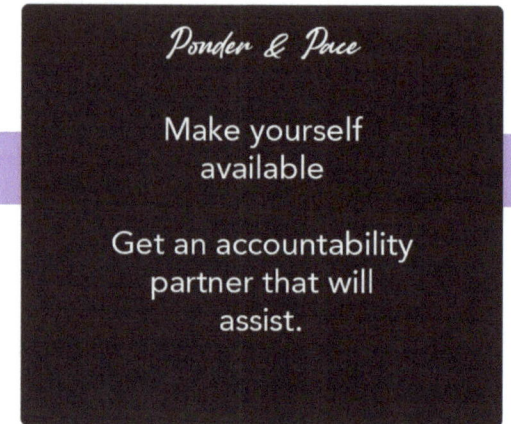

This heroine was Rahab, and her story begins in Joshua during the invasion of the city of Jericho by the Israelites. Jericho was a large Canaanite fortress city, and it was directly in the path of the Israelites, God's chosen people, who had just crossed the Jordan River. Before proceeding into battle, Joshua sent two spies into Jericho. The king of Jericho heard two Israelite spies were in the city and sent troops to search for them.

Although Jericho was a fortress, the less fortunate people lived outside of the walls of Jericho. Rahab and her family were poor and ran a tavern right outside of Jericho's walls. Rahab was known to be a prostitute, and many men visited the tavern. One evening, two strangers came into her establishment. She was a smart woman and realized that these men were spies. She knew there would probably be an attack on Jericho and would have to take action to survive. She told the spies how the citizens of Jericho had been fearful of the Israelites ever since the Egyptians were defeated during the Red Sea saga. She agreed to help the spies escape if she and her family were spared in the upcoming battle. Rahab hid the two men on the flat roof of her house, under large bundles of flax. When the soldiers arrived to look for the spies, Rahab told them that they were not there. The soldiers searched the tavern, but Rahab had hidden the spies well. The spies agreed to protect her and her family, but explained that she must hang a scarlet rope out of the window so the Israelites would know which home to spare.

We see a woman who in society's eyes was as low as she could go. She doesn't appear to have many friends, if any at all. We see a woman that has done whatever she needed to do to make ends meet. She doesn't have a lot of money and I am sure if we would have a conversation with my girl, she'd probably change a few decisions she had made. We see her as an outcast, but she didn't allow any of that, nor what people might say stop her.

Rahab answered the call. Rahab had to make a decision. She had to put together a plan and put it into action. She decided to open the door and allow the spies to come into the tavern. She believes in herself enough to move forward. She then hides them. She didn't allow her fear to hinder her from doing what was needed to secure her bag, to set her family free. I'm sure there were some fears that she had, but they didn't prevent her from moving forward. Despite the conflict between Joshua and the king, she believed that she could help the spies, and she did. She risked her life to protect the spies, but even more to reach her goal of taking care of her mother, father, brothers, sisters, and their families.

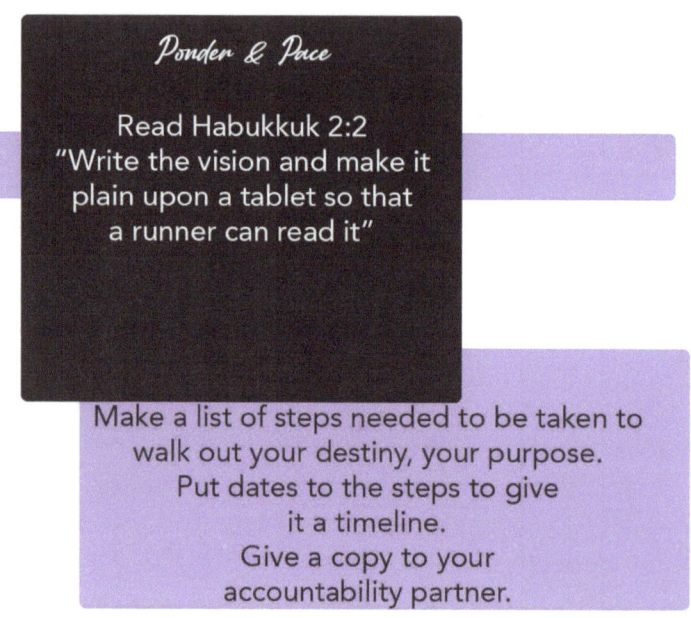

Ponder & Pace

Read Habukkuk 2:2
"Write the vision and make it plain upon a tablet so that a runner can read it"

Make a list of steps needed to be taken to walk out your destiny, your purpose. Put dates to the steps to give it a timeline.
Give a copy to your accountability partner.

WHAT COULD HINDER MANIFESTATION

Who wants to have made it this far and not walk in or see the full manifestation of what you were created to do? After all the work, you must see the outcome. How many people have you helped? How many people's lives have you touched because you are in your purpose, your determined end? How far are you from fulfilling your dreams? And most of all, how fulfilled do you feel? You must keep going, you must work past even the things that may slow you down.

Life-altering events can be difficult at the best of times. Even when we anticipate them, look forward to them and plan for them, it can still be challenging when they roll out. What about when something happens that permanently changes your life in ways you would never want? Now that's a whole other story altogether! If it was a sudden and unexpected change, even worse. This just seems like life hauling off and giving you a big punch in the face. It hurts, causing internal injuries to your heart and soul.

If it were the ribs, knee, or any other physical part of the body that got damaged, no problem, off to the doctor we go, most of us willingly and without hesitation. If it is the psyche that takes the blow; the mind, soul, and spirit, there is much more reluctance to seeking help. Many of us do never even acknowledge consciously that we have been hurt. We bury it instead.

I am here to inform you that it is impossible to live life without getting hurt physically. No matter how careful you are, you will get scratched eventually. Something will get broken or bruised. And you will need physical healing. It is also impossible to live life without getting hurt emotionally. No matter how careful you are, you will get misunderstood eventually. Promises will get broken, and dreams will get bruised. And you will need emotional healing.

You know what emotional hurt feels like. Maybe you're all too familiar with it. Your heart bears scratches of neglect or abuse. And at some point, or another, you've been lied to or talked about, or abandoned. Someone turned their back on you, criticized you, or ignored you.

> **Ponder & Pace**
>
> List anything that may hinder manifestation.
>
> Put actions steps to remove the things that may hinder you.

You know what emotional hurt feels like. Maybe you're all too familiar with it. Your heart bears scratches of neglect or abuse. And at some point, or another, you've been lied to or talked about, or abandoned. Someone turned their back on you, criticized you, or ignored you. And in those moments, emotional injuries were inflicted.

But unlike our body, our heart does not always automatically heal itself. And if healing doesn't take place, we become an emotional mess of accumulated injuries. We deserve more than that, and that is the importance of healing. We are whole beings, not a bunch of separate snap-on parts put together like little plastic building blocks. We are physical, cognitive, emotional, spiritual beings with all four aspects intricately woven together to form a unique mesh that we call me. With all of our uniqueness and strange reasoning and ideas. If one part of us is hurt, the whole is affected. When one part of us is not assisted to heal or heal properly, our whole being suffers. True respect for ourselves, and us being authentic, grows out of the acknowledgment of our wholeness. Only then are we able to recognize that in order to care for ourselves, we have to care for all of us.

Healing is important to the manifestation, since we may not be obedient or may not pursue something that looks familiar to what or who hurt us in the past. It may not be the same person or the same situation, but because it looks like or may represent that situation, we walk away from instead of towards causing us to walk toward death, not destiny. We don't see it that way since we are blinded by the bruises and brokenness of the past, of the things we aren't healed from, causing us not to be whole. When we are made whole, we can fully use our gifts and talents in any area because regardless of how familiar the situations look, I have learned that the trials and tribulations taught me how to walk through that. The trials were steppingstones to reach this manifested end. When made whole, we can go back and deal with those that hurt us and not do it in malice but in true love. We can then walk away knowing that we are moving forward.

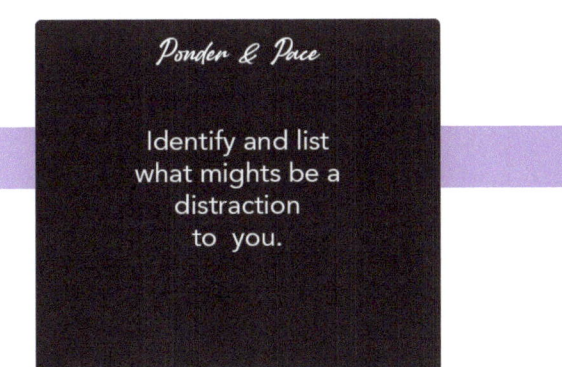

Healing also comes at different levels. It may appear to be linked together like a chain. We may get rid of one of the links in the chain, but not realize that we have so many more links left in the chain. That doesn't mean progress isn't being made, it just means there is still work to be done. Healing will happen at every level and many times in our lives. Just as we are constantly growing, we have opportunities constantly to heal. We must always stay open to the opportunity to be healed. It may appear to be involving the same situation. For example, in a divorce, you may have forgiven the partner, the things that were said, done, and how the situation made you feel. Years later, you realize that you haven't forgiven yourself. Regardless of what the situation is, we must forgive ourselves!!

GOD'S MANIFESTED PLAN

You have reached the part where you get an opportunity to see the manifestation of the plan. Manifestation is defined by an event, action, or object that clearly shows or embodies something, an outward or visible expression, a sign of an ailment, proof, or evidence. I'd like to call it the manifestation of God's plan. It is my belief that the desires we have, the goals, the dream, and the calls are all a part of His perfect plan for our lives. It may take us years to see it, but I believe that every trial, circumstance, and situation is used to create steps for this journey, this race. I believe that the mistakes and the stumbles strengthen us along this journey, and we learn from all of them but ultimately those experiences groom us for the call, the people, and the places we will encounter as a part of who we were predestined to be.

My definition of manifestation is the appearance of something, the miracle, the magic of something, or that "ah-ha" moment when everything finally comes together like puzzle pieces. All the pain suddenly has a purpose. The moment all the hard work, all the training, all the hard places all make sense, or at least you can see them differently. That position you worked so hard for, the business you worked tirelessly to build, the relationships you desired and worked so hard to accomplish, the house, the car, the feeling of peace and contentment, the desire to be where you were predestined to be all along, it all has finally come to past. However, you are not quite done. There is more to come, but you can rest in the fact that manifestation happens. Manifestation takes place all around us. We just have to learn to recognize the areas that this has taken place in our lives. The proof or the evidence of the work that we have done in various areas has given visible signs. For some, it may be the marriage that you desired, for an example, the smile on a woman's face when her husband appears, showing how much she loves him. Or the child that you asked for, a raise on your job, the dream job that you always wanted; the career, a home, and the list could go on.

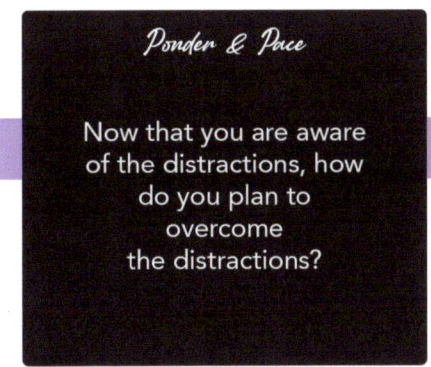

Ponder & Pace

Now that you are aware of the distractions, how do you plan to overcome the distractions?

Now you may be saying that I don't have any of those things in my life as of yet because these are physical items. If that is you, then let's look at how manifestation may feel. It may feel like a sense of peace about a situation or the fact that you are no longer in that situation and that may bring you joy. You may feel grateful or appreciate something or an affirmation that was given to you.

These things appear to be small to us, so we don't recognize them as evidence of the manifestation of God's perfect plan in our lives. We magnify the pain it took to get to this part of the purpose, of our purpose, but I want to point out the fact that these are steps to your destiny. These things groom the personality that God has placed in you to be whom He created you to be. These experiences will be the testimony or the evidence for you and others that manifestation took place.

We are always growing and evolving. We are taking the ordered steps for us to become. However, you may reach the purpose you were called in one area of your life, but things may still be grooming you or working in other areas. For example, you may be working the job you have always wanted and are enjoying life there. You are being promoted, making good money, and love all the people you work with. Now you may be able to see God's plan manifest for you.

Now the talent or gift that you are using in your job may overflow to another area of your life. Your administration gifting may be needed in your church; your counseling degree may be needed in small groups at church to assist others to be healed; the manifestation of your degree or talent in your job has now overflowed into other areas. Why? Because that too is all a part of what your destiny encompasses. The overflow pushes you into your destiny.

I guess what I am saying is that the chase for destiny is ongoing; it is constant. We are always chasing destiny as we move from one level to the next in this life. As I have heard many say, level up, as we level up, we grow, and we are constantly chasing destiny. As we chase after our determined end, then we serve the purpose that we were created to do.

> *Ponder & Pace*
> Read Joshua 1:9 "I've commanded you to be brave and strong, haven't I? Don't be alarmed or terrified because the Lord your God is with you wherever you go."
>
> Choose at least one step from your list and start it today.

As we reflect on Rahab, we can take a few lessons from her. She didn't procrastinate. If you read her story thoroughly, we see that after she was given instructions about the scarlet rope; she acted. She placed the rope out the window immediately. She wasn't going to forget or let the opportunity pass her. She was decisive and clear about her goal; what it was she was attempting to achieve and went after it.

Rahab teaches us to look for and see opportunities in every situation. She knew the importance of trust. The spies promised to save her and her family on the condition she didn't tell their business. She didn't share their business; she used integrity, and as a result, gathered influence. She did not require anyone to motivate her; she was self-motivated.

Rahab fulfilled her destiny. She did exactly what she was created to do. She may have made some mistakes along the way. She may not have always made the "right" choice, but she kept moving forward. She worked through her fears and allowed her fear to push her into position for her destiny.

Just in case you aren't familiar with Rahab or her determined end, ultimately, she married Salmon, an Israelite from the tribe of Judah. Her son was Boaz, the husband of Ruth. Joseph, the adoptive father of Jesus, is her direct descendant. Rahab was no longer viewed as an unclean prostitute, but as one worthy through God's grace.

Now, you beautiful, fearless, bold queen, stand up, hold your head up, and straighten your crown. You are a masterpiece, and you are ready to chase your determined end. You are to run after that dream, that goal. Answer the call and do it with the assurance that even with the mistakes, all is well. You get up and continue the race. Remember, the race isn't given to the swift nor the strong, but to the one that finishes the race. Run on my friend, run on my sister… run on Queen!!

PRAYER:

Dear God, please forgive me for the times I've been carrying burdens and troubles all on my own, so loaded down with cares I won't let go of. Would you help me to release those things that weren't intended for me to hold on to? It's hard to let go. It's hard to forgive others for those times they've hurt me. It's difficult to fully trust again sometimes. And that shows me I don't have the faith in you that you've asked me to have. Fill me fresh with your Spirit and give me the faith to believe that you are forever true to your promises, that you are fully trustworthy.

I ask that you open doors that no one could shut; I ask that you close the doors tightly that never need to be opened again. Help me to stop wrestling, help me to stop trying to work it all out in my power and on my own. I am tired and weary. I am drained. I am facing discouragement at every turn. Yet I believe you are a miracle-working God. I believe you are a God that will allow things to manifest, and I thank you that you are fighting for me today, even behind the scenes where I can't fully see. I thank you for the manifestation of the things to come and the things that have already shown in my life.

Thank you, that you see the big picture, that you know far more than I am even aware of, and I trust you in that. Thank you for the gifts and talents you have given me to assist in the purpose, the destiny that you have for me. I pray for your will to be done and not our own. I choose to find rest and joy in you today. Thank you for your goodness and favor over my days. Thank you, that you give me great hope and purpose for the future. I lay it all down before you, again. Thank you, that this race isn't given to the swift nor the strong, but to the one that continues to the end. I decree and declare that I will finish this race. In Jesus' name. Amen!

Scripture: Joshua 1:9

Ponder & Pace

Congratulations! You have reached the end of the devotional and the finish line is in sight. Take this time to head to your social media platform where you will introduce the Chasing Destiny you, the goal accomplished you. Introduce the one that has completed this devotional and on the journey to destiny. "Speak those things that be not as if they were." Romans 4:17
You may not have made it just yet,
but you are well on your way.
Keep going!
#ChasingDestiny

One More Call

There is a story about a Samaritan woman in the fourth chapter of John. The story begins as Jesus and his disciples are traveling from Jerusalem to Galilee. To make their journey shorter, they take the quickest route through Samaria.

Tired and thirsty, Jesus sat by Jacob's well while his disciples went to the village to purchase food. It was about noon, the hottest part of the day, and a Samaritan woman came to the well at this inconvenient time to draw water. During his encounter with the woman at the well, Jesus broke several Jewish customs. First, he spoke to her even though she was a woman. Second, she was a Samaritan woman, and the Jews traditionally despised Samaritans.

To fully grasp the story of the woman at the well, it is important to understand who the Samaritans were—a mixed-race people who had intermarried with the Assyrians centuries before. They were hated by the Jews because of this cultural mixing and because they had their version of the Bible and their own temple on Mount Gerizim.

The Samaritan woman Jesus met faced prejudice from her community. She came to draw water at the hottest part of the day, instead of the usual morning or evening times, because she was shunned and rejected by the other women of the area for her immorality. Jesus knew her history, but still accepted her and ministered to her.

When Jesus revealed himself as the Living Water to the woman at the well, his message was strikingly similar to his revelation as the Bread of Life: "I am the bread of life. Whoever comes to me will never be hungry again. Whoever believes in me will never be thirsty" (John 6:35, NLT).

By reaching out to the Samaritans, Jesus showed that his mission was to all people, not just the Jews. If you have read this and you are thinking I have a past too or I'd love to do this with the guidance and relationship of a God who will love me in spite of me.

It wasn't about what the Samaritan had done; it wasn't about the men, the mistakes she had made, the lack of friends she had, or even her ethnicity. Those things didn't define her. It wasn't about what the other women were saying. At that moment, it was about Jesus and about the gift that Jesus was attempting to give her. If you continue to read, she was hesitant and even attempted to use deflection, but she was able to see and receive the gift that was being offered. She, too, chased her destiny. The Samaritan woman became a vibrant and successful witness for Jesus Christ.

She is never named, yet her encounter with Jesus is the longest between the Messiah and any other individual in the Gospel of John. Representing the lowest of the low — a female in a society where women are both demeaned and disregarded, a race traditionally despised by Jews, and living in shame as a social outcast

— she not only has a holy encounter with Christ but also receives eternal salvation. And her testimony convinces an entire town to believe, too.

I want to leave with you knowing that despite what has been done, said, mistakes that were made, rejection, guilt and just feeling alone that Jesus is there always. He is forgiving, loving, and a redemptive God. He loves us so much and just like the gift He gave the woman; He wants to give it to you. He offered her the gift of redemption and that may not be your issue, but for you, it might be the gifts or the gifting that you aren't sure of that Jesus is offering you. Just like Jesus was there for the Samaritan woman, He is there for you to guide you in the gift, the call. He met her right where she was. And best of all, not only does Jesus accept her, but He accepts us, and He is right where you are, too.

Prayer of Salvation

Jesus, I am sorry that I have lived my life without you. Please forgive me. Come into my heart. I am a sinner and I need you to be my Lord and Savior. Jesus, I believe in You. You are the Son of God. I believe you died on the cross for me. You took my place and all the punishment that I deserved. I believe you died and were buried, and on the third day, you rose from the dead. I want to follow You and be Your Disciple. I want to learn how to live the new life that You have for me. I receive You now, Jesus, into my life, and I give all of myself to You. Take me just the way I am and make me what You want me to be. Thank You, Jesus, for saving me. Fill me now with Your Holy Spirit and teach me everything I need to know. In Jesus' name, I pray, Amen!

www.ingramcontent.com/pod-product-compliance
Lightning Source LLC
Chambersburg PA
CBHW042236090526
44589CB00006B/76